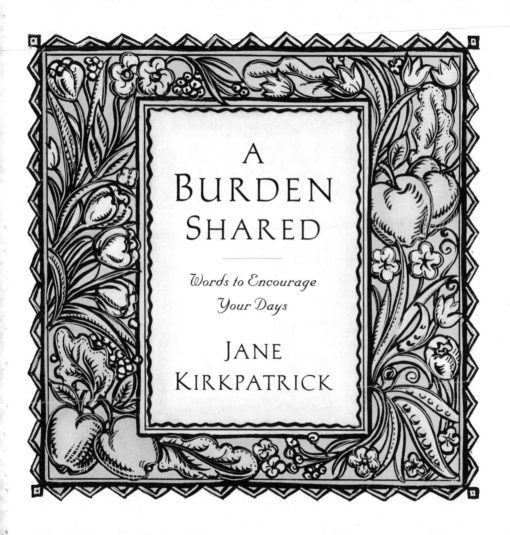

A BURDEN SHARED

*Words to Encourage
Your Days*

JANE KIRKPATRICK

A BURDEN SHARED
published by Multnomah Publishers, Inc.

© 1998 by Jane Kirkpatrick

International Standard Book Number: 1-5767-3-315-7

Illustration by Pearl Beach
Design by D² DesignWorks

Scripture quotations are from:
The Holy Bible, New International Version
© 1973, 1984 by International Bible Society,
used by permission of Zondervan Publishing House

Printed in the United States of America

For information:
MULTNOMAH PUBLISHERS, INC.
POST OFFICE BOX 1720
SISTERS, OREGON 97759

Library of Congress Cataloging-in-Publication Data:
Kirkpatrick, Jane, 1946–
A burden shared : words to encourage your days / by Jane Kirkpatrick.
p. cm.
Includes bibliographical references.

ISBN 1-57673-315-7 (alk. paper)
1. Consolation. 2. Encouragement—Religious aspects—
—Christianity. I. Title.
BV4905.2K55 1998
242' .4—dc21   98-11273
                                       CIP

98 99 00 01 02 03 04 05 — 10 9 8 7 6 5 4 3 2 1

*Other Books
by Jane Kirkpatrick*

HOMESTEAD *(Nonfiction)*

A SWEETNESS TO THE SOUL
Winner of the 1995 Wrangler Award for Outstanding Western Novel

LOVE TO WATER MY SOUL

A GATHERING OF FINCHES

This book
is dedicated to Jerry,
who on this earth
has shared my burdens most
and to Alice Gray,
my editor,
for walking beside me

Contents

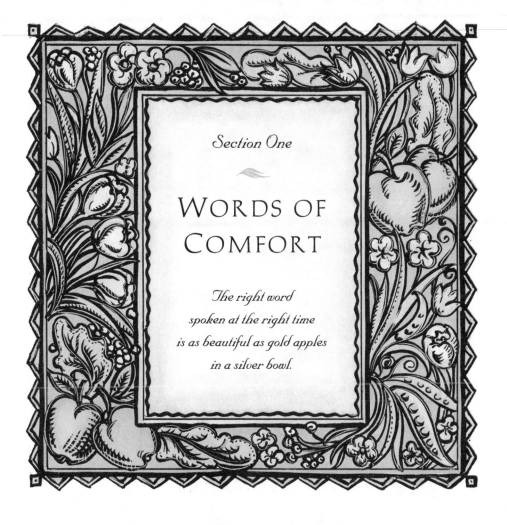

Section One

WORDS OF
COMFORT

*The right word
spoken at the right time
is as beautiful as gold apples
in a silver bowl.*

The right word spoken at the right time," says the proverb, "is as beautiful as gold apples in a silver bowl."

I want to give you words of wisdom, offered to open your clear and perceptive mind.

I want to give you words of comfort, shared so you can feel the love so many have for you, to lift and buoy you in your swirling waters.

I want to give you words of joy, spoken to make your spirit laugh and see the brightness of a future filled with those who care.

I want to give you words of endurance, words to inspire you and support you through this time and yet to let you know I have great confidence in your courage and your competence.

I want to give you words to nourish your soul, place golden apples in your silver bowl.

If I could find a way to be there, I would come; to listen while you told of what you'd done to help another, how your hands had touched and washed and tenderly directed. I would hold you while you spoke of powerlessness and pain, wipe your tears when you related that all you did could not hold on to what life gave you and then took away.

I'm not standing beside you now, not holding you in person. But I am with you. My arms embrace you. My prayers are sent to give you strength so you will know that you are loved and yes, admired too, for all you did and do. And it's my deep hope that what I send to you will be enough to see you through.

You are more to me than "friend," and yet I know no other word that says as much. You are a treasure in my chest of wealth. You honor energy, close connection and commitment, trust and hope. Your care stands firm; fired through the heat of change and distance, troubled times and tears. You are free of the veil of judgment or the sting of chastisement while you hold me in your mind. And if you could, I believe you'd hold me through the night as well and let me cry.

All that you would do for me, I would do for you. It is how we treat our priceless treasures. I would be a treasure to you.

The word "abide" once meant "to cover,"
to offer protection in the way an eagle's wing
folds over its young.
Today it means "awaiting" too,
and signifies both a willingness and
a promise to endure.
I want to be a friend that abides with you today
through prayer and the process of
folding you into my heart.

The porch swing hangs from a ceiling chain. Shaded by the roof, its wooden slats, worn by posteriors and time, feel cool. Dogs lie at our feet, heads cocked and curious at our moving laps. We watch white-faced cows and calves puddle in the sun beside the river. Chukars chatter on rimrocks across the ravine. The smell of sage rises with the breeze.

Then we notice something new: before us grows an apple tree we didn't plant ourselves! It springs from the ground where we fed the mules their apples.

The view from the porch is pleasant, though we rarely took the time to notice until we sat to swing. Animals sleep. The river flows on. A tree grows without effort. Our souls are fed.

In these tornado times it can be difficult to find a place to sit and swing and let your soul be soothed. And yet it's needed: to notice what can happen without effort, that even in the midst of turmoil, tranquillity flourishes.

If you do not have a porch swing in your life, a place to sit and rest and gather nourishment, please come sit on mine. Together we can find tranquillity.

I heard about it and felt the wash of sadness that must have cascaded over you when you learned; a sense of drowning, suffocating, and yet a pain so searing it could have been a thousand bee stings striking all at once.

If I could stand beside you now, I would; to deflect the waves of pain you don't deserve nor can you stop for now. I'd tell you that this pain will pass and hope that you'd believe me.

You'll breath again, remember when it did not hurt so much and inhale strength from memories as you take each breath. Until that moment comes when you begin to live again, I pray my heart, less broken, will beat soundly for both of us.

It's in the little places where grief hides, jumps out to surprise us when we least expect. It's hidden in the scent of a sweater, a perfume, a food, the sound of the river at night. Grief huddles, then leaps into the flush of a flower, the melody of a song shared, the touch of a hand to a cheek. It explodes a memory thought put well away; it's the little things that bring back the pain.

My care for you in this troubling time is but a little thing in the scheme of what you face. Its packaging is small and may seem insignificant. But it is sturdy, strong, and never-ending. I bring it so you can hold it as assurance that the wounds will heal and you won't always hurt so deeply when grief surprises you from its hiding places in your world.

A winter wind whipped past her through the parlor door. Before her, women sat and stitched. Their worn and wrinkled fingers pulled together pieces of her past cut into little squares: a child's worn dress, a bedroom curtain, a flowered tablecloth (with the berry stain her husband made one holiday cut out and now discarded). Dozens of memories they patched together.

That day the women did the final stitching, making perfect edges then tying the tiny strings to keep the stuffing behind each quilted piece. They sewed the single-colored backing down. The comforter, completed, would keep her warm through winter's winds.

What comforts are the memories, the patches that mark the past and then are held together with the stitching hands of friends placed over solid backing. Surrounded by the fondness, we recall the memories, let them nourish us, keep us warm, and give us needed sleep; knowing in the morning we can set aside the quilt, rested, still wrapped in comfort.

In these difficult days, I give my comforter to you. May the memories you wish to savor wrap themselves around you, stitched together by the hands of friends.

They say that anger is an afterthought, one that follows loss. To calm the anger, to turn it into something purposeful and strong, the loss must first be counted and remembered, not trivialized or disclaimed. Only then can loss be searched and finally forgiven. Only then can loss be grieved and allowed to change us.

Your loss is grievous. No words can fill the space you have nor ease the impact of the wound, and yet I'd spend the night with you to try to find the words to ease, the touch that heals. I suspect we would discover once again that life is not fair. Life only is.

You are special to me. The most that I can offer is to help you make the claim against your disappointment, lament its happening and the loss, and help you live again.

They shared a neighborhood and street, these friends; shared good memories, good times. When each wife became a widow within weeks of the other, they shared in mourning, too. The women made a pact that no hour would be too late to wake the other when the memories and loss became so great that only a friend's embrace could get them through. No need to call ahead, just knock on the other's door. Each agreed to give in this special way.

One night the grief became so great it woke her, the anguish so real it sliced her troubled sleep. In her nightdress, she fled into the darkness seeking solace at her neighbor's door. She did not make it. Instead, she met her friend midstreet, equally seeking, reaching for the comfort found only inside understanding arms.

I would be that open to your needs, night or day, no need to call ahead, no need to arrange. And I know that you would be there to share my mourning too. In that way, our lives would meet, our shared healing soothe life's wounds.

What makes you precious is that you are both beloved and rare, unique in your spirit, devoted to care of me and others whom your life touches. Like the mythical flower, the purple amaranth, you never fade; even though time passes, even though winds flow. The sun may beat unmercifully but your vibrancy endures. You are what friendship is for me: a model of acceptance without condition, care wrapped in the petal of gentleness, watered with the refreshment of love.

Now, if you'll permit me, I have the chance to care for you, to be that never fading flower that rejuvenates your life in this shadowed time.

You may feel far from the shoreline, adrift without oars. Does it feel as though you're sinking, just a rock dropping to the bottom with no hope of notice, never mind rescue?

As you swim toward the safety of the beach, please remember: even rocks dropped into the center of a pool eventually make their mark on distant banks.

Your touch reaches far beyond you.

My hands stretch out to you to lift you up and pull you out so you can look back and see the imprint that you have made upon the lives of others.

J A N E   K I R K P A T R I C K

In a Central American country, Korean students came to rebuild some widows' homes. A girl stepped out to share the evening with stars and sleepy volcanoes and found before her circles of fires. "You come to give us help in a dangerous time," her hosts said when she asked about the flames. "We wish to cover you with our fires."

The sight and sentiment so moved her, she stepped back inside to wake her friends who joined in the watch. The young woman brought her violin out and in the clear dark night began to play "A Mighty Fortress Is Our God." The strains of hope and confidence lifted to the heavens through the night, friends warming friends by protective firelight.

Like a violin played in a faraway land, inside my heart the strains of courage and determination sing for you. I offer warmth on a cold evening, light when life seems dark, and the promise that I'll stand beside you against oppression while we thank God for our protection.

Legs in casts, unable to walk, we watched while others performed our work. How could we repay them, neighbors and strangers who fed our cattle and tended our fields? We who were so self-sufficient just sat, healing, while others could act.

"Repay us?" said a rancher when I shared my lament. "Oh no, this is our gift. You honor us when you accept offers of aid. When you're mended and healed you'll have a lifetime of opportunity to pass it on."

A lesson learned while watching and holding: the best we can hope for in our time of need is to accept help from others and then pass love along.

In a rainbow, each shade of color arrives as a refraction of the sun through rain or mist. At night, a rainbow can form too, if moonlight and moisture mix. The colors are more muted then, a darker velvet version of each daylight hue; the pillowed brilliance comes from the sun's reflected light against the moon. The rainbow's colors at night are stunning in their splendor.

It is in reflected darkness that the depth and breadth of color truly shine, regardless of how muted they might at first appear.

In this dark time, the colors of daylight are still there, bright and beautiful. Color lives in darkness too. May you find the rainbow of the night and recognize it as all the more remarkable because it is reflected light.

You who give so much to others:
may you find your own strength, faith,
and flexibility reflected in the lives
of those you cherish.
You reach beyond yourself;
you lend a helping hand.
You live your faith each day.
You are a warm and nourishing light
in what is sometimes a dark and dreary world.
I am grateful
for the warmth the light of your life
has given me.

Beethoven introduced character pieces into classical music, though his publisher discouraged "little" compositions. He urged, instead, efforts on prodigious works, the symphonies and lengthy opus.

Beethoven ignored the admonition. Instead, he wrote both the complex symphonies and what became known as "character pieces," the scherzos, the trifling "bagatelle." Shorter pieces contributed to harmony and resonance in music in new and unexpected ways.

Who's to say that interwoven, complex works of art contribute more or stay longer in the memory? Who's to say that shorter songs of rich and vibrant tones leave less behind when their melodies cease? Each is important in the music of our lives, no one the greater than the other.

As you face this troubling time, I hope you listen to the music of what was, however long the symphony, however short the composition, and remember all the deep and enlightening notes. Let them linger and encourage you, a reminder that you will hear music again, sometime in the future.

*A friend
holds your hands
in their thoughts and
their prayers.*

Section Two

NEW
BEGINNINGS

*There is
a time to mourn and
a time to dance.*

irst the "why" arrives. Why me? Why this? Why now? Then comes the anger or regret, perhaps the bargain of how it will all go differently next time, if only this or that could happen now. Then comes the wrenching sadness like a fog that threatens to never lift. Finally, acceptance appears. Like the slow development of a photograph, the image becomes clearer until we recognize it for what it is.

Knowing, acknowledging, accepting, we can move on. We may step back a time or two, on an anniversary date, at the scent of something that brings this moment and this loss to mind. But the pain will lessen as it moves through time.

Such is the promise of a new beginning bound into the process of grief.

*There is a time to mourn
and a time to dance.*

ECCLESIASTES 3:4

His broken ankles and hip, her shattered foot and arm left them helpless for a time, the airplane accident taking its toll. One day the casts came off, and they thought they'd dance for joy to ballroom music in the city the way they had before the clatter and crash of metal against pavement. But they couldn't. Too much pain, recovery not yet present though the bones looked stronger and the X rays showed the breaks had mended. Deep healing takes more time.

A year passed. On a Saturday morning, wearing blue coveralls, he asked her to dance there in the living room with the dogs lying surprised at the feet of their masters' strange movements. Gently, he began to swirl her about the room, his wide hands holding her close to feel the slight adjustments he should make. She accommodated for how his broken hip had healed; he compensated for her shattered foot and her now fused arch.

Their arms held differently, aware of each other's needs, they now could dance. They eased around the living room, smiles reflecting in each other's eyes while music played. A slight adjustment, accommodation and realignment and they danced on. Isn't that what life's about? Some fixing and fine tuning over time, aware of breaks and the patience needed for mending.

The Acoma, indigenous people of North America, are known for their pottery of great beauty and strength. What distinguishes their pots from other Pueblos' is the mix of the clay.

Grandmothers search the desert for shards of pottery once formed, fired, used, and then discarded. Lifting the broken pieces from beneath the sage and white sand, they grind the old shards into powder. The potters then mix the old powder with unfired new. The two clays—the old and the new together—are molded and when fired become the strongest pottery.

So we are formed, if we allow it. Old powder from our past experiences once thought useless, broken, lacking value, can be combined with new ones and through the fires of life, can give us strength.

I wish for you this kind of strength.

It's said that 80 percent of what we communicate comes, not through words, but from gestures: the tilt of our head, the lift of an eyebrow, how our arms lie crossed, where we place our gaze. Even the inflection of our speech carries meaning far greater than the words. I can say "I love you," but it's how I act upon the words that tells you if what I say is true.

I wish that I could be there with you so you could see the way I feel. My arms are open to embrace you, my ears block out the sounds of this world so I can hear only what you wish to say. My eyes are prepared to shed tears with you. My fingertips will wipe the wetness from your cheeks. We will sigh together and take one deep breath and start again. It is a message of my care that I communicate in this difficult time.

Wheat harvest in the west has its own season of beginnings. Grain is planted, nourished by the rainfall and hot, steady sun. Green stalks bend into wind. When the heads are ready, the fields turn slowly gold. Hawks dip and swoop above the combines. Grain pours into trucks that deliver the bounty to storage elevators, and finally it is loaded onto ships and tables thousands of miles away. The planting has come full cycle. Almost.

Seed enough to plant again is kept behind. The weeds are culled by fingers so only what is wanted remains. An abundant harvest would be remiss without plans for reseeding for the future.

People need that privilege too, a season promised for reseeding.

In this time that seems so far from harvest, I will help you find a seed worth planting, the promise of tomorrow inside a harvest of today.

Rain on high desert juniper and pine leaves the freshest essence. A clean aroma, one heralding a new debut, it cannot be matched by tree-shaped deodorizers or spray cans of scent. Those are mere imitations of the wondrous, real thing.

As you seek your new debut, a place where pain and powerlessness are left behind, look for what is real and lasting. My care fits there, a fondness for you that bears no imitation but is meant to give refreshment in this difficult time.

Towering clouds ease across the sky, draping barren hills with thick, dark shadows. Or are those knolls left bereft from a wildfire, all foliage burned, nothing remaining behind but black? Perhaps the clouds camouflage the raw remains of ravaging flames. Who's to say what the shadows tell: covering a wound or offering shade?

A higher plane, a different angle and I can see. The hills are fine and green. Only the shadows have made them threatening.

Move with me to another view, past this temporary time when things look bleak and black. I will walk with you to a place where you can see past shadows and find beneath them the promise of vibrant green.

One hundred years ago, people often spoke with flowers, sending handwritten scripts through bouquets. "I will not give thee up," the slender columbine said. "One may smile and be a villain still," spoke the small but flashy sweet william. "May you taste the sweets of true friendship," it was said the rose meant.

During challenges, it was the quiet chamomile that spoke the loudest. Used as tea to help one sleep, to treat many inner organs inflamed and sharp with pain; chamomile, with its dissected leaves, also meant encouragement to another when going through troubled times. "Cheerfulness in adversity," the fragrant white flower said and urged the recipient to keep hopeful through the hardship.

I would send a fragrant bouquet to you today, one fruitful with both flowers and thoughts. Press their image and their message in your mind. As you walk through difficult days, let the flowers speak of promise, friendship, and reassurance.

In Guatemala, all roads lead to the presidential palace in the heart of the capital city. Inside the president's receiving room, beneath a gold and crystal chandelier, lies a circle of inlaid wood. Slender strips of mahogany mark the place where all kilometers of twisting roads begin their journey in this Central American country. Anyone lost among the vibrant greenery or deep ravines need only find one paved road to follow, and they'll be returned to the center of that president's room.

I know it feels as though you're lost today. Your roads appear twisted and in places overgrown with uncertainty and fear. Look for the markers that say others have walked this road before. My care for you is but a small sign. An even larger hallmark is the knowledge that each life lived in faith forms from the Center, Christ. If we choose that Center, it is a place where rest and strength and great compassion live, where forgiveness, hope, and healing walk abreast.

I hope you'll seek that place and find your way back to the Center.

A valley, after all, is simply land surrounded by partnering hills. Without the hills, there'd be no vale. Each depends upon the other, though hills are given better press. Mountaintop experiences are seen as more desirable than those moments far below.

Valleys have much to offer. They are protected places; far from winds that often buffet, high exposure, or gales that sting our ears and stop our hearing. In valleys, we avoid the blowing sand that pits our faces and forces us to close our eyes. Valleys offer views containing, though not confining. In the shadow of the mountaintops, we can gain sustenance from the soils that line the riverbanks and the stillness of sheltered lands.

You may feel that you're inside a valley now, one suffocating and restricting. But I can see the possibilities in your vale, even if you never see the mountaintop. With ears tuned toward the future and no blowing sand to snarl the view, I would take a tour with you and help you seek mountaintop experiences in the lowlands of your life.

The Paiute people of the Great Basin of North America captured antelope on their annual hunts they called their "charmings." Mounds of grass and juniper branches placed in a circle created the illusion of a fenced corral out in the sagebrush-dotted desert. For days, the people walked the perimeter of the circle and made a larger one around the herd in a figure eight formation. Daily, they tightened up the circles until the antelope were gently moved inside the mounds. Because the herd had seen what looked like fences keeping people in a circle, they did not try to rush between the mounds to seek escape. Instead, the images of what they thought they'd seen kept them confined and ultimately resulted in their demise.

Sometimes we can be charmed, too, and miss the openings in the fences of our past. I would help you recognize the open spaces, see where we can walk through; not to forget what helped make you what you are, but to walk through the difficult days toward better times ahead.

The field's been plowed.
Now that you see it,
you wish that it had been left alone.
You imagine in your mind the way
the field looked green with virgin grass,
untilled.
But the field's been plowed,
and now it's time to plant anew.
Make it the best plowed field ever.
I'll work it with you.
Together we will produce a strong and worthy yield
by accepting all that is and moving on.

"What's done is done," says the octogenarian who lived through a financial collapse, a war, and the loss of a son. "When I find myself clinging to what was, wallowing like an old buffalo in the sand, I give myself a time of day, an hour when wailing about history will have its place. Five o'clock I pick. Just for an hour, though. By six o'clock, I will be done. That way I keep those meddling thoughts in check. They've got to wait 'til five and only then get sixty minutes."

Five o'clock arrives. But instead of giving up an hour to think of what could or should have been, the wise old soul makes a phone call to a friend. He fixes a bowl of soup and savors the aroma of the moment. He pays a bill and mails it; reads a book that brings on laughter; feeds the dog.

"What's done is done. Events cannot be brought back or changed. Only what this moment brings can I command and so I do it," the elder says. "I make the time be filled with what my mind decides will give me strength, not what once was."

The author said her fingernails grew long while writing. She had no time to chew them then. Revisions were another story. Reworking novels required time to stare at sentences, deciding what to cut, which way the plot worked best. Then began the waiting, wondering if her editor approved. "You can tell what stage my writing's in by the length of my nails," she told friends.

When the final revisions were approved to print, the president of the publishing house sent the author a box and a personal note. "I understand you worry about revision," he said. "I want to reassure you and with these gifts give you a head start on your next novel."

The gift box contained not a new pen or computer disk nor other writer's tool, but a manicure set, practical help to survive the next revision.

You're in the modification stage, full of uncertainty and effort. I hope that the gift of my friendship is strength for your nail-growing times.

You may think your time to flower has passed, that too many years or hard events will keep you from blooming more. But it is the lengthening of days that brings the bloom, not the endurance of the plant or even the vigilance of the gardener, though each contributes. It is additional light, added exposure to the nutrients of sun touching each plant's unique code that produces the flower, and later, the fruit.

When you see the yellows of chrysanthemums, or spring's lilac blues, please remember that you share this in common with the plants: blooms occur when living things are nourished by extended exposure to God's light. May today be the day you truly bloom.

Surviving, said women in a research study, meant living with loss, overcoming hard times, managing being different, and learning to put difficult things behind you. Their strength, they said, came not from enduring the hardships themselves, but from *how* they survived them. Especially important was the sustenance of close relationships, like going to a well for water.

Creating a place where one could feel at home, accomplishing a valued task and allowing themselves to feel satisfaction, all gave these people strength. Being able to gather memories and reflect on life's patterns seemed to grant vitality. They told stories of decisions made, past regrets, details of the lessons learned, the role of faith and family, and the fellowship found in the shelter of everyday life.

You are that kind of strong person. You will survive this hard time.

Section Three

GIFTS THAT
ENCOURAGE

*You give me encouragement,
bring laughter to my days,
and light the lamp for me during
my darkest nights.*

T he disease takes away my sincerity," my sister said. She can't control her tone of voice or how much air she sends across her windpipe. Some days her eyelids close and cannot be opened without help. "It doesn't let me say the things I mean. I need another voice."

Some days we all need another voice, someone to listen, to understand meaning, asking questions only to find clarity and direction. "I would be your voice," I say, and so she lets me, two now needed where one was once enough.

I would be your voice, too, someone willing to put self aside to hear and speak only what you wanted; to intervene in your world, to touch the lives of those you love just the way you wished. I would put myself aside to make you heard, extend your sincerity, and consider it a privilege and a gift that you would trust me to speak for you, to let your hopes and wishes be heard inside my voice.

51

Fields of corn are promises kept, the currency of care. Every silky, slippery thread that tops the stalk and lends itself to sun and rain leads directly beneath the shucks to the slender cob and an individual kernel. Without the wispy, almost unnoticeable silk, each tiny kernel could not exist, would not fulfill its promise. It could not be fertilized, its genetic code would not compute. On the cob, a bare spot would remain where a plump and moisture-laden kernel was meant to be.

I think the corncob says we can have assurance that the God who designed the cornstalk down to the tiny details has the power and will to care that much for us. Every kindness, every helping hand, every moment when another reaches out to touch our spirit with nourishment and warmth are simply silky threads meant to bring inspiration deep inside the souls we clothe beneath our skins.

Thunder eggs. Oval-shaped and heavy, they're ancient lava bubbles filled with mineral clothed in the grayest stone. They're often found by one rounded edge seen poking out through dense layers of rocks and sediment dropped eons ago. Not much to bring notice to themselves on the outside, but rockhounds seek them as fine treasures.

It's their insides that surprise. Cracked open, thunder eggs reveal colors not even hinted at by their rough exteriors: blues and rusts and vibrant purples, whites with crystal-looking centers. Fired by the volcanic explosion, the outside served as mere casing for the inside; the part that, when polished, outshines the brightest jewels.

I know that like the thunder egg, what's inside of you is what will matter. Your vitality and strength, your ability to persevere despite external force is what will see you through. May the center of the thunder egg bear the message of the confidence I have in you.

The morning pain makes me call out her name—not "Pearl," the name given her seventy-nine years ago upon her birth, but "Mother"; that solid, sturdy, civilized word that must mean "one who cares."

I am not your mother or your father; neither are you mine. Yet I know what love is because of how you've cared for me, offered sustenance and sacrifice, persevered when less than family would have walked away.

I would mother you now, as you struggle for a time, and extend the sturdiness that a loving family shelters.

I watch you struggle,
seeking meaning and strong comfort.
Some of what you hope for seems to flee and fade away.
I ache for you then,
wanting the most for you.
I wish for you the deepest reach,
your arms opened,
your heart prepared for His strong love.
It is what I know will give you strength
and truly fill your soul.

55

To you,
whose heart belongs to others,
who gives with joy and ease,
who seeks forgiveness without agitation
and trusts God for all provision:
you carry the survivor spirit
in your heart.

It's said that agents seeking counterfeit currency spend hours and hours in study of authentic bills before they ever peer on fraudulent cash. The most important lesson, they say, is in knowing inside and out that which is genuine and valued before being exposed to flimsy imitation. Knowledge of that highest standard must be certain for imitation to be exposed.

I would urge you into "real"…a life of care and giving, one led by God to use your gifts in service of another. You are no imitation but are genuine, authentic, and distinctive.

Music weaves its way inside and out in strangely interwoven ways. The woman said her chickens laid more eggs when she played Brahms to them throughout the night. At our old dairy, the Holstein cows gave up more milk with music playing. Babies are said to calm themselves to strains of Mozart or Chopin, even in the womb, and then select their favorites when those same songs are heard again in the nursery. At the other end of life, music brings old toes to tapping; feet and hands that might not have stirred for years pick up the beat. Music soothes and moves.

I hope you find the music of your life, that you will give yourself permission to take time to listen and be rested by the tones and tempos that best suit you. In troubling times, let the melodies make you more productive and take you back to memories of restful infancy; and forward, to anticipate the joyous dances of old age. Listen closely. I hear a song being played for you.

It has the illusion of calm, the word "pastor" does, evoking images of peace and placid pastoral green dotted with the fleecy white of tranquil sheep.

But the word means "shepherd" in the German language. It's meaning draws strength from the caretaker, not the surrounding sheep or soil. The shepherd is a being who tends but also fights off predators. The shepherd aggressively seeks out wayward lambs. He reaches out to protect by preventing potentially poor choices.

Others might look upon your world today as placid and calm and cannot see the turmoil rolling inside you, the potential problems you are sorting through. I would urge you now to call upon the Shepherd in your life. He will pastor you through.

Family. It has a dozen definitions, but it's taken from the Latin word *famulus* meaning "servant."

I may not be of your lineage, your bloodline; or one you'd call your kin, but I am willing to be family, your servant, in these difficult days. It would be my gift to counsel, listen, bring you nourishment and help the throbbing in your head fade away by my presence, my good will for you, my wish to ease your days.

My German grandmother
translated the word "depression"
as "strong courage."
May you discover strength
in this time of depression,
and may the wisdom of your years
unveil your valor, too.

Its needles never fall, and it produces berries bright and blue that catch the snow in winter and the scattered shade of spring. It grows in soil most other trees find too desolate and barren. The juniper's roots are deep and reach for miles. Its gold and sienna twists of wood grain produce prized and valued lumber.

Only junipers that have withstood strain put forth such beauty and uniqueness. I see you as the hardy juniper who has withstood years of wind and drought and winter's caustic cold. May the juniper's twisted trunk and branches promise worth and treasure, prizes granted only by endurance through tough times.

They call out, those geese, not because they're passing on the wrong side. They honk, those geese, not to bring attention to themselves, to complain, nor mark a territory, or so researchers say. No, those migrating waterfowl call to encourage their companions, to cheer them on.

Can you hear me? I am there, sometimes from a distance, sometimes overhead, maybe out in front, but always encouraging you. That's what friends are for, to find the language of the call and speak it. I hope today you hear me through your discouragement and pain.

You have walked beside others with compassion and care. Your stride was broad enough to stimulate their efforts, though they were sometimes tired; yet small enough to stay abreast. You encouraged success.

I am willing to walk beside you now in your time of trial. I'll let you set the pace and encourage you to the end.

American poet Robert Frost once wrote "good fences make good neighbors." It was what his neighbor said. Frost disagreed. His neighbor felt a fence respected boundaries but offered joining too, as neighbors worked together in the spring to keep the rock walls functional and firm.

As the poet, I'd prefer no fences between us, no rocks piled so high I cannot see the worry on your face, the way your shoulders bend with the weight of stones you carry, what tension hides within your hands.

But if you create a fence, I will respect it and not cross without invitation. But I hope you keep the barrier low. For then I can reach across, make my offer. If you accept it and balance me as I step over into your world of sadness or distress, I will bring my presence and my prayers. I will bring confidence, too, that while our fences stand between us, they need not separate us. I will do my best to keep the fences low so they never block the gifts friends bring, both helpfulness and hope.

Like waves
that tease a child's toes,
joy reaches out to you.
It may seem tentative at first,
but the promise of peace and
predictability will arrive,
carried on the crest of sorrow.

If I fix it, I take away your chance to use the tools you think fit best to repair it as you'd like. If I fix it, I deprive you of the knowledge you can think and act creatively, find inspiration in the depths of disappointment. You might well resent my meddling in this building project called "your life."

I won't be a fixer because I can't and shouldn't. Neither will I let my eyes belie a patronizing attitude about your lack of builder skills. But I will loan you tools and the wisdom of my experience and be your finest "go-for" ever, if you ask. I'll "go for" nails and saws, sandpaper and tape, whatever you decide you need to remodel this hard time into a living space of open, soaring ceilings held firm by strong, protective walls.

Section Four

MOMENTUM

*May time
travel over you without
leaving tracks.*

Y ou don't have to climb the mountain today, only find the footholds that will greet you in the morning. You don't have to graduate today, only take that first class. You don't have to write a novel, just pen a paragraph. Somehow we seem to think we must be large enough to finish before we first begin.

We gain by just beginning, take on new strength with each small step taken, even if we have to later change our course. Clarity and direction rise from the swirl of indecision; courage and potency appear through the malaise of unworthiness and woe.

Your faith need not be strong enough to finish, only adequate to embark. We can take the next first step together.

71

Even out of emptiness our souls can give just by letting others walk beside us, accepting what they have to offer. In that giving, we receive nurture for our journey and the promise of companionship through disappointment and pain. In times of trouble, you often step out to walk beside others with kindness and care. May you know today that someone wishes to walk beside you. You give a gift when you let them.

Given as a gift, the blue tarp once provided shade. Later, it covered irrigation pumps put up for the winter. When it began to shred, it offered filtered light, a flash of color over the dog run. The wind whipped it further, and it should have been discarded as the blue strings drifted in the breeze. It was useless, but we didn't toss it away.

In the fall, when the wind blew leaves off a nearby tree, we discovered new meaning from the tarp. Hanging in the tree that towered over the kennel were blue nests. The birds had taken what we'd thought useless and formed new baskets of color in the poplar tree.

That's what love is, I think: to take what might have seemed unworthy, past its prime, and turn it into nurture.

My care for you is wrapped within the blue tarp of your life. I have great hope and promise, and, because no winds are buffeting me, I can see potential. When all the leaves are gone and you feel stripped and bare, I'll be there wearing blue, offering my love to you.

Even strong,
deep-rooted trees must bend in the wind
or be torn from the soil.
Your world is buffeted by gale forces.
Please don't feel you must stand so straight
into the wind you bear too much.
Please don't think that strength
cannot hold gentleness and rest.
It can.
Lean into me.
Together we can weather this.

The clay felt slick and smooth against my skin. The thumpa-thumpa of my foot turning the wheel played a soothing melody. Mud and water together in a lump, that's how I'd start while imagining the bowl or cup I'd somehow make.

My efforts fell short. My cups listed to the side; my bowls all wore leaning lips.

"You haven't centered the clay before you begin," my instructor told me. Then she put her hands over mine grasping the ball of clay and helped me feel the center of the spinning wheel, that place where all pottery grows to become well formed. I felt it through my fingertips, up to my arms and somehow deep within. My next pots had sides as I'd imagined in my mind.

I've never been where you are, never endured what you've been asked to bear. But if you will let me, I will place my hands on yours and help you find your center. I'll help you grow deep wisdom not from my experience but from my love.

Students learning the art of basket-making have a tradition: they give their first completed basket away, often to their master basket teacher.

I've wondered about the custom. What kind of person would I give my first efforts to? Someone who would not judge my work harshly. Someone comfortable finding good woven within bad, who sees promise and potential hidden inside effort. A person familiar with expectation and encouragement, who will tell me that what I've made is worthy just because it comes from me.

And why would I want to give my first effort away? Why not wait until improvement shows within the weaving of my basket? Perhaps to prevent discouragement that might come from being reminded daily of my first feeble efforts.

No, I'd surrender it because it is the greatest gift of love to relinquish the first fruits of our creation; the greatest gift of trust to offer someone the tentative imperfection of our hands. To give away a portion of ourselves that's less than perfect is an act of courage and devotion. It's what we do when we admit our faults and ask forgiveness. It's what happens when another accepts us as we are.

Daily, we make first baskets woven of our experiences, our hopes and disappointments. Daily, we have a Teacher willing to accept our efforts. Today, seek the master basket teacher and know the joy of relinquishment, the peace of acceptance as you are.

The carpenter's coping saw is formed of steel forged as thin as a child's ribbon. Used to fit things into tight places, like cabinets into corners, the blade must be both strong and flexible. Too strong, and it will splinter what needs to be fit; too flexible and unwanted gaps will remain. To cope successfully, the blade must demonstrate both strength and flexibility.

The coping saw speaks to life as well, how we must learn to cope. We need strength and flexibility, knowing when to stand firm and when to bend a bit, back off to let God make the final fit.

Every farmer knows that when the time is right and the field is ready, it must be planted. No priority is higher on the "to do" list when that day arrives. All other activities must be set aside.

You have a field to plant. Set aside the other tasks that consume your time and get the seeds, fire up the tractor, and begin. What lies unfinished now can wait. We all must focus on the goal of planting when the field is ready or we will have no yield.

In this troubled time, look to the farmer and the fields. Know what you hope to harvest in the months ahead and place the seeds now in the readied soil. I will help you plant and if you wish, wait with you to help bring in the harvest.

*Jesus grew in wisdom and in stature
and in favor with God and man.*

LUKE 2:52

As a physician, the apostle Luke would have been familiar with the four facets of our lives where we must heal. Wisdom means to use our mind and memory to manage strong emotions so we solve problems rather than let passion propel us into impulse. Stature says to tend to our body and our mind and what we put inside. Growing in favor with mankind speaks of nurturing if we're to live in harmony. And how we grow spiritually, the way we move away or toward God, will tell if we're locked in conflict over power and control or available for change, abundant living, and forgiveness.

I hope your life, now filled with tension, will find direction in Luke's prescription: a description of where to find the answers for your stress and Who will help you wipe away the turmoil and emptiness.

Brody, the black Labrador retriever, jumps and barks with the sound of food pellets rolling into his bowl. His excitement would make a stranger think he'd never been fed, a fact his ninety-six pounds belies. Later, lifting the leash turns him inside out, he anticipates his walk. The sight of a mud puddle lures him to splashing ecstasy. The dog's joy honors everyday events. He isn't troubled by repetition and routine. He craves it.

In difficult times, the dog is a reminder that joy explodes from the familiar, not as tedium, but as triumph. It is hidden in the simple and routine. May you recognize it as the sun warms your face or raindrops wash against your cheeks. May it enter your senses in the sweet smell of an infant after her bath, in the sweep of leaves from the driveway, cool tile against your bare feet.

May you find in your daily tasks today, not the drudgery of obligation, but the exuberance of a Labrador. The common in a time of turmoil can bring the greatest peace.

I braced myself each time we drove down our driveway's roller coaster dirt and gravel grade. "Sixteen percent" my husband said it was. "Steep" I called it. As I sat beside him, I'd push my hands to the truck roof, thrust my right foot straight ahead, and jam my left foot on the center mound as if to brake. I asked for slow and steady, a safe pace to straddle two-foot-deep ruts washed there by heavy rains. One day we started slowly, then rushed forward, careened between sagebrush, over ruts and rocks, our heads (and the dog's) hitting the roof, knocking glasses askew while I shouted at my husband to "Slow Down."

"I can't!" he shouted back as he reached to turn the switch. At the bottom of the hill I caught my breath with plans to chastise him for terrifying me with speed. But before I could, he said through teeth clenched tightly: "Jane. Take. Your. Foot. Off. The. Accelerator." And so I did, my own appendage having slipped and slammed the truck to seventy, all while I blamed him.

It is a message with some meaning for me. To gain control, I sometimes push too hard. Instead of warding off destruction, I cause more. Instead of owning what I do, I look for someone else to blame.

You may feel you're careening down a roller coaster grade without control. See how you've braced yourself. Make sure your feet cause no harm. And if you need to, call me. I know how to share humble pie at the bottom of life's roller coaster grades.

Weeping may last
for a nighttime but joy
comes in the morning.

PSALM 30:5

In Oklahoma City, a bomb exploded and left behind still forms of children, mothers and fathers, grandparents and friends who would never laugh nor love again. Survivors' grief and pain were telecast throughout the world, and ordinary people joined in mourning, in expressing horror and our anger.

A year later, a limousine driver told of how the town was healing as he put his tip into a separate jar. Any child injured by this tragedy would have hope for their future, offered by the people of this all-American city. Chief executive officers, cab drivers, school children, and parents could all contribute to a college fund for survivors. Something good, something long lasting and meaningful will come from a bombing of the innocent.

Ordinary people with good will have moved their anger and their mourning, taken tragedy and transformed it.

In your troubled times, I would help you find a catalyst for hope wrapped inside your tragedy, one that will turn your mourning and your anger into triumph; your despair into the promise of a future joy.

In rolling wheatland country, the fields of green that turn to amber before harvest are marked in difficult terrain with patches of sagebrush, rocks and weeds. "Scab" patches, the ranchers call them, places too rugged to farm, given a name that sets them apart. A thing cut out with no hope of harvest.

Yet in those patches hide the mule deer and their fawns who wait for dusk to nibble on new shoots of wheat or barley at the field's edge. Pheasants nest in sagebrush shade, their young safe and close to grain. Lizards warm themselves on rocks. The grasses hold back water and prevent wind erosion of the soil. The sun sets on them, the brown and green breaking up the miles of treeless landscape marked by rows of grain growing to the far horizon.

They are a thing cut out, pared away, rough and often rejected, and yet offer protection and a harvest all their own.

In your seemingly endless landscape of distress, seek the yields promised in the surprising places of your life.

The tipple was a necessity in coal mines on the coast. Built at the mine entrance, it weighed, sorted, and cleaned the ore arriving from shafts dug into hillsides like rabbit warrens. Soot-covered rope riders, usually boys, rode atop the ore carts out of the mine, jumping off at the tipple. Black ore tumbled into the usually wooden two-story structure. The tipple did the organizing and analyzing, taking something raw from earth and assigning it a value. How much the ore weighed helped determine its worth. Its density and size mattered too. Without the tipple, confusion reigned. When the tipple was down, no ore could be processed, no values assigned.

In these troubled times, I wish a working tipple for you, one that lets you sort out what has value and what does not. On days when the ore carts come too quickly, may you take time to work the tipple of your mind, putting precious energy into what has greatest value and letting smaller, insignificant things drop into slots marked "later" or "never mind."

There are mosaics in a marriage, patterns that define uniqueness and reflect the seasons of a couple's years. The places they fished or golfed, the stories told of first meetings and falling in love, hard times, and change. Such marriage stories preserve tradition and transport a family's cultural value and beliefs from one generation to the next. Patterns. They tell stories and offer meaning.

Misfortune, hardship, grief, and trouble have their patterns too. From them we learn to seek the messages inlaid within the worry and the work that comes with living. Wisdom appears, emerges from the lessons scratched across the slates of our lives.

Strength lives inside mosaics too, within the patterns layered upon life. I would be a part of your mosaic, help you find the pattern that will tell you what should happen next, what step to take, how to proceed. It is your pattern, your story. You are the author of the next chapter.

The wider the river,
the more shallow its depth.
It's a given most fishermen know.
Keep your banks straight and narrow
so you can draw deep.
That's where the biggest fish grow.

Section Five

DREAMS
AND RISKS

*May neither the errors
of your past nor the terrors of
your future keep you
from walking where God's
spirit leads you.*

You risked, stretched yourself, and some might say, you'd failed. But if all we chanced promised perfection, there'd be no need for human beings, we'd just use machines to decide the direction we should take.

You proved your humanness and hopefulness, and I admire your choice to risk no matter how others rate results. You inhaled life and exhaled inspiration.

We called it our "refuge," one hundred and fifty acres of rattle-snake and rock along a meandering river. We told few of it, not sure how they'd accept a plan to leave convenience for sagebrush and sand. It was a dream, a belief we had that we belonged there, for whatever reason.

Some weeks before we moved, an acquaintance confirmed it. "Don't know what this is about, but you kept coming to my thoughts today along with the word 'refuge.' Figured you should go there, wherever that refuge was."

Refuge. A place of protection, a place sought out for help.

We moved to Starvation Point. Others have come too, to find a sense of healing and renewal. But the refuge didn't grow from the shadows of the rim-rocks nor from the cooling shade of sage. We found refuge in our willingness to step out upon a cloud of faith, believing we would not fall through.

I know you're struggling and uncertain. Perhaps I've been sent to carry words of "refuge" to your ear. It lies inside a rock of faith, a place of fine protection with God's strength to see you through.

The capacity to dream and take the dream from wispiness to real lives inside hardy spirits. A commitment makes it easier to withstand the storms that blast our sailing ships or the fires that consume the things we've cared for in the dark of night. A firm decision pulls us like a beacon toward it, so disasters only change the path we take, not the destination.

But even thieves can keep commitments. It is commitment to a goal that nourishes others that matters. So the farmer feeds his cattle and survives the blizzards and frostbitten feet because others count on him. A mother works two jobs, yet rises in the night to make her children's lunches and then studies for her college classes, all to give her family future opportunities. They are hardy people whose commitments serve others.

You have made a worthy commitment. Now when the dream seems distant, when turmoil threatens, let commitment be the light you follow through the gloom. Do not mistake this darkness for the final destination.

Knowing what we control and what we don't will make us hardy. When disappointment swipes, when abandonment and loss come riding by, when the river rises out of season or drought steals all the harvest, hardy people become powerful. They ask what action they can take, how to respond; not "why me?" "why this?" "why now?" They spend little time assigning blame. They waste no energy in accusation, not because they might not win a legal battle or find someone else to fault, but because both blame and self-recrimination rob a hardy person. Lament and blame keep hardy people from their commitments. Victims lack the power of a victor.

Hardy people ask what they do command. They can't call back the act that brought the misery and strain, but they do control their attitude. They put the difficulty in perspective.

I know it seems much is now beyond what you control. Still, I hope you see your choices, however small and insignificant they might appear. I hope you choose to become a hardy spirit.

Challenges, hazards, opposition come to all of us. Some hand us personal pain or business strain. Some ask us to change the way we live or work, who we share our time with, whisk away a resource or support we've come to count on. Some make us think we've lost all that we've worked for or believed in. Challenges can be small detours or significant disasters.

Hardy people meet challenges head on and perform a face-lift. Instead of a calamity, they describe a challenge as an opportunity, a chance to learn something they otherwise might never have known—about themselves or what truly matters in their lives. They call challenge an invitation, not a summons. They recognize it as a teacher bringing needed instruction, even guidance, the chance to deepen wisdom or expand inventiveness. Each challenge faced and placed behind is a triumph promising confidence that one more important step has been taken toward the goal.

May you find today's challenge the opportunity you've been seeking, not the tragedy that you feared.

First comes the vision, the dream to work toward. Then instructions follow, how to proceed. Materials arrive, sometimes even before directions. What's available may even redefine the dream we seek. Helpers and interpreters are provided, people who have struggled through the difficult places and can help us see why we've run afoul and how to turn it into treasure. Then come the alterations, the challenges and disappointments that require adjustments to the pattern to make it fit. And in the end we have the piece of work, our vision, now in hand; but it is not yet complete. Not until we stitch the piece of Grandma's lace or attach that brass button that makes this finished pattern uniquely ours.

Like the prophet Jeremiah, I believe that God has a plan for each of us, a good dream, not one to harm us.

You're still designing your life's pattern. Let me help. I'll share materials, interpretations and hold your hand through alterations and join in the celebration at the end.

"For I know
the plans I have for you,"
declares the Lord,
"plans to prosper you and not to harm you,
plans to give you hope and a future."

JEREMIAH 29:11

Kelpies are stock dogs. Short, close to the ground, a kelpie can still jump six feet into the air. Loyal, duty-bound, they're used for herding sheep and cattle. Because they're light and yet can leap, they clear the fences between pens and run across the backs of sheep to where they need to be to keep the peace, leaving behind no evidence they stepped on fleecy backs.

With cows, the little dogs nip at the nose or heels of animals one hundred times their body weight or size. They are fearless, taking on predators known for fierceness but not backing off, snapping at air with their powerful jaws. Yet at day's end, they lie about with children without bother. The kelpie knows its duty and direction and trusts it has been given all it needs to do its job.

I wish for you today the confidence of the kelpie; the clear commitment to your task, the courage to face foes twice your size, to soar over barriers and fences, and yet to tread so slightly upon others they never know that you've been there; accomplishing your mission, panting, happy with success at your day's end.

The special bed was made to take away the pain caused by serious burns. Into white sand that formed the mattress, air was pumped to make the person lying on the hospital bed feel as though they rested on a cloud. No ankle or elbow ever felt a pressure; no back nor heel bore pain. In fact, patients felt nothing on this bed, and that became the problem.

Life without boundaries and definition, even though it was free of pain, caused restlessness, disorientation. Agitated by the lack of feeling, of not knowing where one was in space, recovery was hindered instead of helped.

No white fluffy mattress exists to take your pain away today. If it did, you too might end up disjointed, disorganized, and muddled. Perhaps the pain you feel is setting boundaries for your being. Please hear it speaking of both hurt and the promise that you will heal.

Bones of the greater Canada goose are porous and light, designed to hold the air they breathe inside and keep them airborne. They fly farther and remain longer because of these featherlight bones. The bird's engineering and design, its capacity to take in air and flush it through its body is a marvel and an inspiration.

"Inspiration" means the act of breathing in.

Be inspired today. Take a deep breath and let it fill your lungs, course through your arteries to feed your body and your brain. No shallow gasps, but a deep intake of breath, an inspiration.

You will fly higher and go farther than you ever thought you could for we, too, are engineered in marvelous ways.

The warning of a flood means look for higher ground.

Today, I'm standing where it's safe and dry. I'm not affected as you are by the rising waters. I can see them, but they do not threaten here above the banks. Look for me. I'm reaching out to you. I'm standing where the ground is stable. I can see beyond the flooding waters to where the world looks familiar, recognizable, and more predictable. Some ground has been washed away; new soil deposited to rebuild a once fragile field.

I have saved a place for you, knowing when I face my flood, you will do the same for me.

Higher, solid ground is what a friend can offer in a flood. Advance a new perspective. I give that now to you. This flood will pass, but I will still be here to stand beside you as we rebuild together.

Though we do quite well for months moving about our world, rolling across the floor to reach what we want, we never stay there. As infants and toddlers, we're driven to be upright, to reach for trees, to grasp so we can find the world and make our mark upon it. No amount of falling makes us decide to see only from our knees. We're built to risk and try again.

Though we may do well picking ourselves up after a fall, nothing heals us faster or makes the next step toward independence easier than when a steadier, stronger hand reaches out to comfort and encourage.

I offer my hand to you as a reminder that though you've fallen, you'll stand again, driven to be upright. Though you're wounded, your knees scraped and scratched from reaching forward, you will soon heal. It is the promise of childhood and a necessary part of being human.

Do butterflies in our stomach just before we give a speech make us speak with more conviction? Do sweaty palms just before the airplane trip make us listen better to the messages designating exits? Does value live inside the anxious times?

Perhaps we were never meant to be complacent. A little apprehension gives us cause to act for our survival and perhaps to care for something other than ourselves.

I know you feel discontented today, full of dread and wonder; and you may think your goal is to eliminate all stress, to be disconnected from all turmoil. But disconnection never raised a responsible child, never cured a rare disease, never built a business or a nation. Perhaps surrender is the goal: surrender to what we can't control and surrender to the little twinge of nervousness that makes us act for change. You can make a difference, not despite your anxious moments, but because of them. I can hardly wait to see how creatively anxiety will act out in you today!

The western cottonwood tree grows tall and firm and bears a thick trunk to support wide-reaching branches graced with leafy shade. Growing beside rivers and streams, they offered ready resting places for pioneers, for grazing cattle, and, in later years, as fuel to heat a settler's home.

In spring, the seedpods dropped their fluff to wind so abundantly it looked as though the trees were snowing. Often, the ground turned white with pillowy drifts beneath the trees.

The wind alone was not enough to make the seed take root. Something more was needed. The cottonwoods needed floods to nurture new growth.

I hope that this distressing time in your life is but a necessary flood: not meant to take away or destroy all that you are or have become, but needed to bring on richer things required for more abundant times; so, like the cottonwood, what you have to offer does not die out.

Artists often say they feel exposed when they perform, read their works, or hang their paintings in a gallery. But musicians, poets, writers, painters all agree, the risk's a worthy one. The exposure of our deepest selves can be the gift that touches others, brings a healing moment, directs someone to a place of strength or comfort, even necessary action.

Grief seems like that too, for some: a painful unmasking of our inner being that leaves us vulnerable and uncovered, fearful others will judge us and then pull away. And yet by sharing it, we have the chance to heal ourselves and reach another wounded soul.

When you come upon that dark place in the night that invites exposure of your grief, please know this: I will stay with you until the morning light, to reassure you that, even with unmasking, you are cared for just the way you are, though vulnerable and exposed.

Section Six

JOURNEY INTO HOPE

*Carry
each other's burdens,
and in this way you will fulfill
the law of Christ.*

The mariposa lily spears the desert sand in June and stands, a purple throat, straight and exposed. It bends but never breaks despite the pressures of hot, sandy winds. Notably, the lily does not bloom each year, responding to some God-given code for its flowering time. But it blooms most often and is the most vibrant following winters distressed with cold and suffocating snows.

As I think of you, I consider the lily and know this too will pass.

At the bottom of the river, I see rocks pushed into piles and ridges by the flood. As the water recedes, mud and slimy reeds collect to make the rocks look gray, uninteresting, alike. I select a few because their shapes are rugged, pocked by other rocks shoved against them in their journey. I take them home and put them in the tumbler.

For days the drumming of the rocks pounding and grinding against each other serenades my daily chores. Eventually, I peek inside the polisher.

Instead of gray or beige I see a stone so smooth it could be ivory or pearl. A gentle band of color swirls through the agate, tumbled evenly to bring out its uniqueness. I would have passed it by except for the dents and scratches that marked its voyage.

I watch your journey full of scrapes and bumps. Marks of the troubling times show well. I can't stop the tumbling, but I can promise that it will cease; and when it does, you will be different. Your qualities of character and vibrant strength will be reflected in the newer, polished you.

Writer Marcel Proust once said the real journey of discovery was not in seeking new landscapes, but in seeing with new eyes. You are on a journey, thrust forward with old baggage from the past, filled with things not even needed where you're headed. Journeys are like that, asking us to pack familiar baggage even though it wears us down.

False starts and detours challenge travel. We may tell ourselves we want off at the nearest stop. Everything challenges our confidence and even our faith. Uncertainty thrives on journeys, seeing through glasses that enlarge the unknown. But destinations are reached, even new and unexpected ones. We can rest. Excitement replaces dread; insight replaces distraction; fond memory replaces anger and daze.

In whatever part of the journey you're on, know that others have walked before you. They've survived, with assurance and surprise. They found a way to see with clearer, new eyes. Until that restful time, let me loan you my glasses as we walk side by side.

"Hope," wrote Václav Havel, "is an orientation of the spirit, an orientation of the heart. It is an ability to work for something because it is good, not just because it stands a chance to succeed. It is not the conviction that something will turn out well, but the certainty that something makes sense, regardless of how it turns out." Havel's view of hope propelled him into prison for his writings but also helped him reach his goal to rid his beloved country of Communism. Today he is the elected president of the newly formed Czech Republic.

Like Havel, your hope is founded not on optimism or Pollyanna-itis either, but in your belief that what you work for is worth doing. It's how you started out, and it is what can keep you moving through the hard times, onward toward your hopeful goal.

Like the slow rising of the river after an early snowmelt in the mountains, it seeps into our lives, unhurried, almost without notice, until the strength and breadth of it covers everything that had once been familiar, makes it different, new over old. No rushing torrents, just slow-rising water, licking at foundations.

Change carries both sides of flooding rivers: it can happen so slowly we don't remember the exact moment when the green alfalfa field became a sea of blue, exposing only islands of green; or it can rush and tear and break apart in seconds everything we hold dear.

What floods and change share in common, these carriers of alteration, is the aftermath, the need to rearrange the way things used to be.

In this time of transformation, I would help you rearrange and give you assurance that one thing remains unaltered: my care for you, whether you're in the midst of a flash flood or a slow-rising river.

We always take more than we need or will use. So what do you pack for this journey? Enough memories of friends and family to warm you in unfamiliar places. Enough time to notice the newness and not be frightened by its unfamiliarity. Enough patience to remember others are traveling, too, and that there's no prize for being first. Pack alternatives. There may be detours. You may not reach your destination on time. And pack a notebook so you can record the highlights of this road you're on, inspiring others to step out into their unknown. Please remember to save room for all the lessons learned that you'll be bringing back, lessons to help me pack for my journeys too.

Each of us feels alone at times, as though we don't belong. We're different, out of step with those around us. It is not a feeling we should fear. It is an indication of our uniqueness and our wish to gather under shelter with another.

Family may fail us; occupation fall short; even our drive for sufficiency, fame, and good fortune will tumble down. Only inside, where the soul opens wide to the Spirit of God, will we discover our true place of belonging.

You do not have to travel alone. Let Him help you on your soul-filling journey toward belonging.

"Survivor guilt," psychologists call it, a sense of unworthiness and pain that comes when one person has outlived another. Such guilt winds a tangled trail marked by grief, both from loss and from wondering why it wasn't us; thinking perhaps some great mistake was made, and we should have been the victim not the victor. We live, not only wondering how to face the day without the ones who've gone, but dealing with our guilt and shame over being left behind.

There are few answers to the questions our surviving raises. But perhaps our living gives a gift. At least the one we loved, who's gone, does not have to bear this double loss. At least the one we loved is free of all the tangled feelings that survivor guilt delivers. It may be small consequence, but one to help us not just survive, but thrive until time lets grief drop behind us on life's trail.

I would take it from you, if I could, tie it up and throw it overboard. Together, we could watch it sink. I might toss a life raft to you, hoping I could help someone I value.

Or would it just be a way of relieving my pain that comes from watching you learn how to handle discord? What message do I send when I throw out a life raft when you are simply learning how to swim? Does it suggest that you might drown without me? Or do I just deprive you of your own discovery that you know how to stay afloat?

Maybe what you need is not a rescuer, but someone cheering while you learn how to breaststroke toward the shore? Hear me? I'm that little voice far in the distance encouraging and rejoicing, and I will be holding the towel as you step triumphant on the beach.

Where mighty rivers meet the ocean tides, the surf is powerful and rough, the place of transition marked with a bar invisible to the untrained eye. Even giant ships with experienced crews and wise old pilots have been known to flounder and succumb to the thunderous crash of waves there.

You are in that place where forces meet, change and disappointment clashing against a wish to keep things in familiar ways and places. It is a power struggle not unlike the ocean tides pounding against rivers.

Crossing over the bar is the hardest part. The crossing does not allow a hesitation once the goal is set. Strain and pain and held breath and prayer are companions on the crossing. On the other side, it will be accomplished, and your ship will move in calmer waters.

I cannot cross the bar for you, but I will be there if you let me. If you ask, I will help you set the course, act as crew or wear the pilot's badge as someone who has crossed through troubled waters and survived. And I will hold you in my thoughts, even after the waters calm.

Gardeners know the time to stake a plant is when it's small and slender, standing straight without a hint that it would ever later bend or break. That's when support is planned for, in the early days of tender, rapid growth that anticipates the winds it doesn't yet feel.

I would be a stake set beside you, to bolster you against the gales, a reminder that you are in a growing place that brings turbulence and whirlwinds with it. I would be a stake that says you do not stand alone.

When someone is going through difficult times, the words of anthropologist Margaret Mead are cast with new meaning. She wrote that the earliest signs of civilization are not the tools or bowls uncovered from the dust of time, but the discovery of healed bones found within the caves or graves of old ones. That a bone could break and heal meant someone had to care enough to carry water, bring in food, fend off enemies, encourage, and daily move the injured from their pallets when the morning pain forced them to call out the name of one who cared.

I will be there when you call the name of one who cares.

It's said that an early meaning of the prefix "com" as in "communion" was "to share burdens." The very word "communion" means to share and exchange, to give and take. It seems that's what we do when we listen to another, truly hear them with our hearts. And when we share the pain and strain of days, we find our load is lighter. We have communed.

"Companion" carries with it meanings such as helpmate and ally, acquaintance and friend. If the prefix rings true, "companion" must mean a willingness to share the burdens, too.

I am willing to share your burdens. For if you let me be your companion during these difficult days, we will commune and share a togetherness meant to lift with compatible compassion.

Shaped like a whirlwind and woven with twists of willows, tules, and tradition, the burden basket once fit on an Indian woman's back. A leather strap across her forehead held the basket steady. She carried only essentials inside, what was needed for huckleberry picking or gathering greasewood or seeds. Few things fit in the narrow bottom; most essentials were visible near the top. Those who walked beside her could see if her shoulders bent with the bulk of her burdens or could tell, even without words, if her head ached from the weight. Assistance could be offered. And so two could walk together toward their destination, helping to bear each other's burdens.

Please place your troubles near the surface so another can offer to share your load. "It's such an old burden," you say. "So heavy. I'm used to carrying it this way." And so you walk stooped over, too tired to set your basket down for just a moment while you run and play. Old habits cling to old burdens. To share them, we must be willing to shift our load.

I see your worries now are deep, that you feel strong enough to carry on alone. I will not rob you of your accomplishment. But I will walk beside you, watch for signs you ache. I'll periodically suggest a shift, select a shady spot to rest. I am here. I am willing. And if you should share your burden, I will be forever honored by this deepest sign of trust.

And when I pray for you and with you, listen to your worries, and then go my separate way, I know you will not be left alone. A Comforter is promised, one to hold you ever after. My prayers are answered by a Counselor's presence even when friends and family are out of sight. You can speak and share at will. You are promised a power far greater than any my meager strength could leave.

My prayers for you are answered by love, unconditional and all sufficient. I leave no greater gift than my willingness to hold you in my prayers. You are there now and will be through this hard time.

The basket is empty,
the load is light.

Notes

The Guatemala Center and the Korean violinist narratives, pages 22 and 40, are told by permission of Wayne Huff, Wycliffe Bible Translators, Central America Mission.

Floral meanings on page 39 are from *Hatchet, Hands & Hoe: Planting the Pioneer Spirit* by Erica Calkins, p. 85. ©1997 The Caxton Printers, Ltd., Caldwell, Idaho. Used by permission.

Stories of being strong on pages 44 and 47 are from "A Heideggerian Hermeneutical Analysis of Older Women's Stories of Being Strong" by Margaret F. Moloney in *IMAGE: Journal of Nursing Scholarship*, vol. 27 (summer 1995), p. 106. Copyrighted material by Sigma Theta Tau International. Used by permission.

Geese images on pages 63 and 102 are from *High Flying Geese: Unexpected Reflections on the Church and Its Ministry* © Dr. Brown Barr, Abingdon Press, Nashville, TN. Used by permission.

The hardiness series on pages 95 through 97 is from "Hardiness: Conceptual and Methodological Issues" by Donna Tartasky in *IMAGE: Journal of Nursing Scholarship*, vol. 25 (fall 1993), p. 226. Copyrighted material by Sigma Theta Tau International. Used by permission.

Václav Havel on hope, page 114, is found in *Disturbing the Peace* by Václav Havel. New York: Vintage Books, 1991, p.181. Copyright ©1990,1991 by Paul Wilson.

Margaret Mead's reference on page 122 is from *Fearfully and Wonderfully Made* by Paul Brand and Philip Yancey. ©1980 Used by permission of Zondervan Publishing House. Available at your local bookstore or by calling 800-727-3480.